FUN WITH

Air and Flight

BARBARA TAYLOR

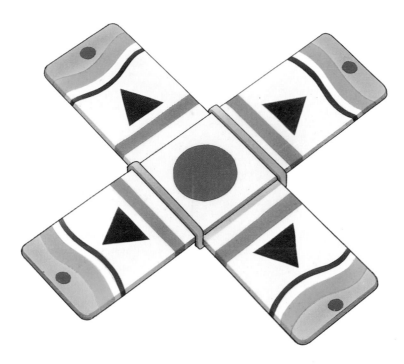

Kingfisher Books

AIR AND FLIGHT

In this book, you can discover why we need air to survive, how the weather is caused by moving air and how machines and animals fly through the air.

The book is divided into six different topics. Look out for the big headings with a circle at the end – like the one at the top of this page. These headings tell you where a new topic starts.

Pages 4–11

Air All Around

Air everyday; breathing air; burning; rusting; air in cooking.

Pages 12–15

Warm Air, Cold Air

Hot-air balloons; convection currents.

Pages 16–19

Air Pushes Back

Compressed air; air pressure; siphons; hovercraft.

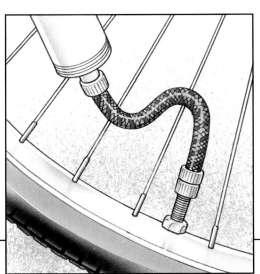

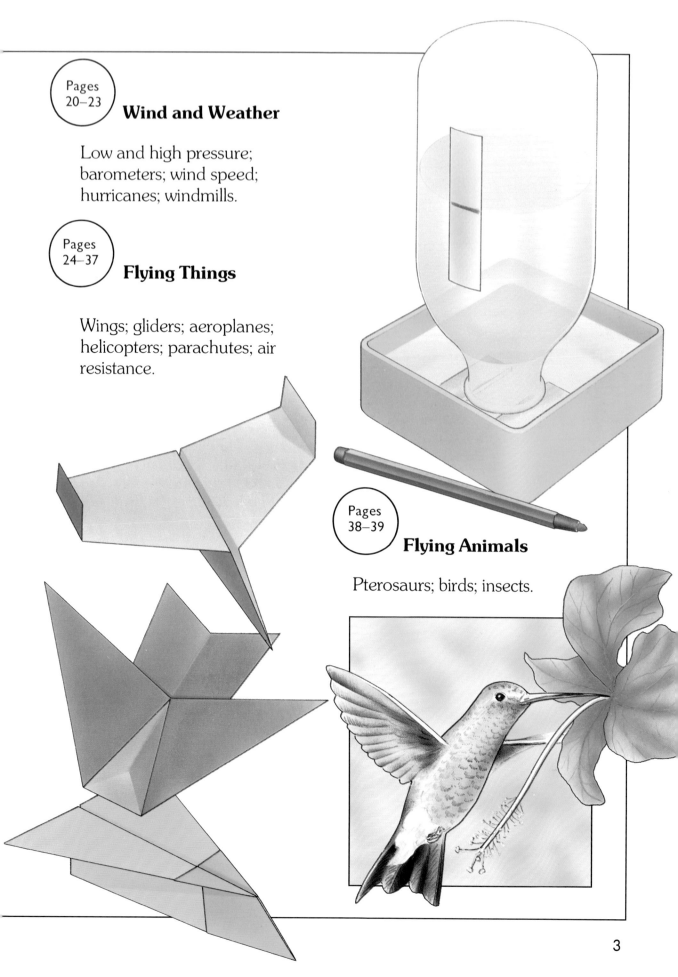

Air is everywhere. It fills the space all around you. It is inside plants and animals, mugs and saucepans, bicycle tyres and balloons. Soil and water also contain air. Because we cannot see, smell or taste air, we often forget that it is there. The best way to investigate air is to look at what it does to things around you.

The pictures along the bottom of these two pages will give you some ideas. How many more examples can you think of? Make up a story or write a poem about how air affects your life.

Bubbles of air in a fizzy drink

▶ When air moves from place to place, we call it the wind. A windy day is a good time to fly a kite. The force of the wind pushes the kite up into the sky.

Blowing up a balloon

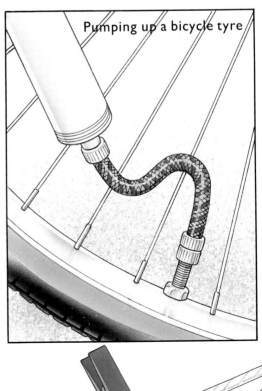

Pumping up a bicycle tyre

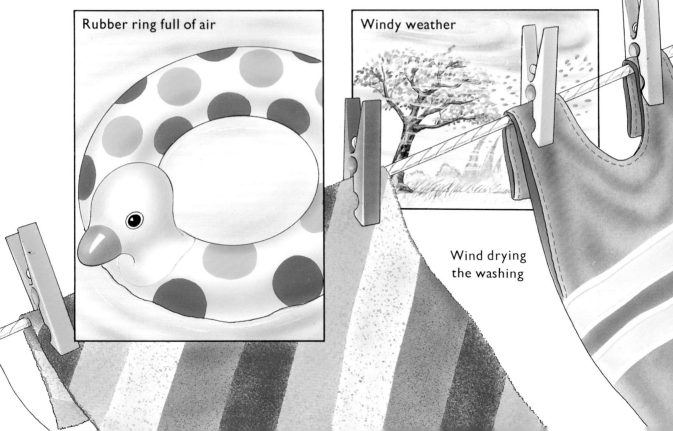

Rubber ring full of air

Windy weather

Wind drying
the washing

 **Breath Power**

Why do you need air? When you breathe in, air is sucked into your lungs. In your lungs, one of the gases in the air – called oxygen – passes into your blood. The blood carries oxygen to every part of the body. You need oxygen to release the energy stored in your food. Without oxygen, you could not survive. All plants and animals need the oxygen in the air to stay alive.

Count how many times you breathe in during one minute. Then run on the spot or up and down stairs for one minute and count again. Repeat the same test after standing still for five minutes or after cycling or swimming. Compare all your results.

You could also feel your pulse before and after taking exercise. To do this, place a finger on the side of your neck or on the inside of your wrist. Your pulse tells you how fast your heart is beating. When you exercise, you need more oxygen, so you breathe faster. The heart beats faster to pump your blood, and the oxygen it carries, around the body.

How big are your lungs?

This experiment will show the amount of air your lungs hold.

You will need:
a large bowl or the bath, a long piece of plastic tubing, masking tape, a large bottle which holds about 5 litres of water, a waterproof pen, a measuring jug or cylinder.

1. Fill the bowl half full of water.
2. Fill the large bottle with water. Stick tape on one side.
3. Hold the bottle over the bowl, put your hand over the neck and carefully turn the bottle upside down. Hold the neck of the bottle under the water. Mark the water level on the tape.
4. Ask a friend to hold the bottle upright and push one end of the plastic tubing into the neck of the bottle.
5. Take a deep breath and blow as hard as you can down the tubing.
6. Mark the level of the water in the bottle when you have finished.
7. Turn the bottle up the right way again. Use the measuring jug or cylinder to pour water into the bottle up to the first mark you made on the side. The amount of water you add is roughly the same as the amount of air in your lungs. It is called your lung capacity.
8. Repeat the test after taking an ordinary breath. How much air do you breathe out this time? Compare your lung capacity with your friends'.

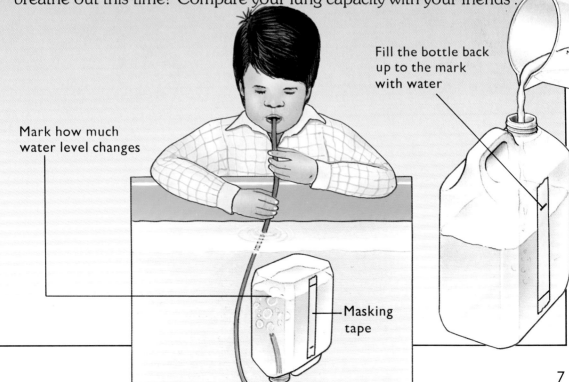

Mark how much water level changes

Fill the bottle back up to the mark with water

Masking tape

Candles and Burning

Things need oxygen in the air to burn. Prove this with candles.

Fix two night-light candles firmly to saucers with modelling clay. Ask an adult to light the candles and put a small jar over one of them. How long do they burn?

What happens

The candle under the jar soon goes out because it uses up all the oxygen. The other candle has lots of oxygen around it, so it burns for longer. Try this test with a larger jar. How long does the candle stay alight this time?

▼ Have you ever noticed flaky brown or red patches on old cars? When iron is left in damp air, it joins with oxygen in the air to form a red powder, which we call rust. Without oxygen, iron will not rust.

Make a Fruit Salad

You will need:
half a lemon, a lemon squeezer, a bowl, a saucer, a chopping board and knife, a spoon, fresh fruit, plastic wrap.

1. Squeeze the juice from the lemon and pour it into the bowl.
2. Ask an adult to help you slice up the fruit.
3. Put one slice of each fruit in the saucer, the rest in the bowl.
4. Use the spoon to cover the fruit in the bowl with lemon juice.
5. Cover the bowl with plastic wrap and put it in the refrigerator. Leave the saucer of fruit out in the air. Which fruit goes brown?

What happens

The oxygen in the air reacts with the fruit and chemical changes make the fruit in the saucer change colour. But the acid in the lemon juice helps to stop this chemical change happening to the fruit in the bowl.

Mouldy food

Leave some boiled potato, orange peel, cheese and stale bread in old saucers on a windowsill. Sprinkle each with water. Which food goes mouldy first? What colour is the mould?

Floating in the air are the tiny spores of a group of fungi called moulds. If these spores land on food, they start to feed and produce more spores. This makes the food turn mouldy.

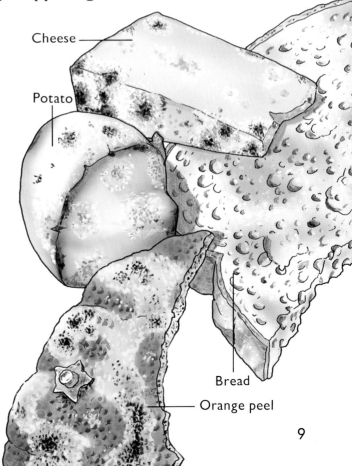

Cheese

Potato

Bread

Orange peel

9

Bubbles in Bread

Use the carbon dioxide given off by yeast to blow up a balloon.

Tie the balloon onto the top

1. Half fill a small jar with warm water and add four sugar cubes.
2. Use the spoon to stir the water until the sugar disappears.
3. Pour the sugary water into the tall bottle.
4. Mix one teaspoon of the yeast with a little water.
5. Add this mixture to the bottle.
6. Use the string to tie the balloon over the neck of the bottle. Leave the bottle in a warm place.

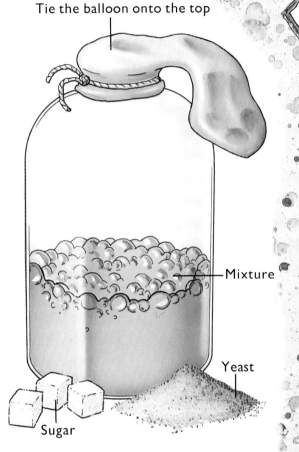

Mixture

Yeast

Sugar

What happens

The yeast feeds on the sugar, grows and gives off carbon dioxide gas. This gas will blow up the balloon. It also makes air holes in bread.

Making Cakes

If you make a cake with plain flour, you need to add baking powder to make the cake light and full of air. Baking powder, like yeast, gives off bubbles of carbon dioxide gas if mixed with water and heated.

10

As Light as Air

You will need:
100 grams strawberries, 1 packet of strawberry jelly, 2 eggs (separated into whites and yolks), 50 grams caster sugar, 75 grams cream cheese.
A large bowl, a small bowl, a fork, a spoon, a whisk or a food mixer, a saucepan.

Mousses, meringues and souffles are light and fluffy because air is whisked into them. Make a strawberry mousse.

1. With an adult, make up the jelly following the instructions, but use only 300 millilitres of water. Leave the jelly in the refrigerator until it starts to thicken.
2. Use the fork to crush the strawberries into a pulp.
3. Ask an adult to help you whisk the egg yolks and sugar in a bowl which is standing in a pan of hot water. The mixture should go thick and pale.
4. Add the crushed stawberries to the egg and sugar mix.
5. When the jelly has started to thicken, add a little jelly to the cream cheese. Beat the cheese with a spoon. Then add the cheese to the egg mixture, together with the jelly.
6. Ask an adult to help you whisk the egg whites until they stand up in stiff peaks.
7. Carefully mix the egg whites into the egg, cheese and jelly mixture.
8. Leave the mousse in the refrigerator until it is set. When you eat the mousse, you will see lots of tiny bubbles of air.

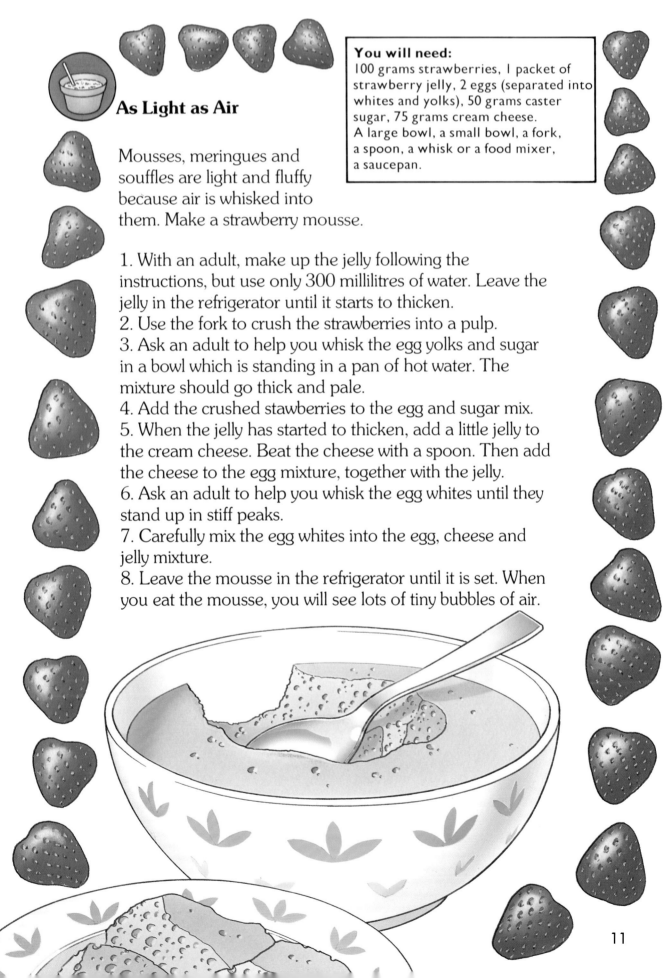

Have you ever watched a bonfire? Sparks from the fire are carried upwards by warm air rising from the fire. As air gets warmer, the particles of which it is made spread out. This makes the air lighter or less dense so it rises upwards. As air cools, it becomes heavier or more dense and sinks downwards again. When heat is carried by the air itself, the process is called convection.

 Falling feathers

Let go of a small feather in different places around a room. Can you find any places where the feather will rise? (A warm radiator is a good place to try.) How high does the feather rise? How long is it in the air?

Bubbles, talcum powder or flour will also help you to detect rising hot air currents.

▲ Air inside a hot-air balloon is heated by a gas flame below the balloon. The hot air inside the balloon is lighter or less dense than the cooler air outside the balloon. As the hot air rises, it carries the balloon upwards. When the gas flame is turned down, the air cools and the balloon sinks back to the ground.

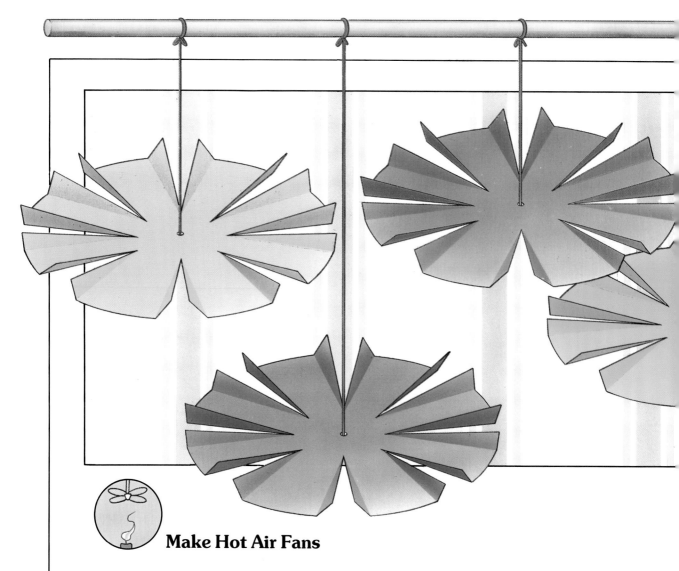

Make Hot Air Fans

These fans will twirl around in rising currents of warm air.

You will need:
coloured paper, a mug or jar, a pencil, a ruler, scissors, thread, tape, a thin stick or piece of dowel.

1. On the coloured paper, draw several circles by tracing around the outside of the mug or jar. Make each circle about 5 centimetres across.
2. Cut out the circles.
3. Fold each circle in half, then in half again and in half a third time.
4. Open out the circles. You should have eight fold lines in each circle.
5. On each fold line, measure 3.5 centimetres from the edge and put a pencil mark.
6. Cut along each fold line up to the pencil dot.
7. Bend up the cut edges, so that each bends the same way.

Cut out circles

Fold up circles

Unfold circles

Cut 3.5cm into the middle

Fold up flaps

Thread cotton

8. Make a hole in the middle of each circle. Push a piece of thread through the hole and tie a knot to stop all the thread coming through. Make each piece of thread a different length.

9. Tie the threads to the stick or dowel and hang the fans over the hot air rising from a radiator.

10. If there is an adult with you, you could hang the fans over a candle flame. But be very careful not to let the paper get anywhere near the flame. And don't forget to put out the candle afterwards.

Can you use a balloon to lift up a plastic beaker? Put the balloon inside the beaker and blow up the balloon. You will find that the sides of the balloon grip the beaker tightly. You should be able to lift up the beaker just by holding on to the neck of the balloon.

This works because air can be squeezed or compressed into a smaller space. The compressed air inside the balloon presses outwards on the sides of the beaker, so you can lift it up. Air pressure can be a powerful force.

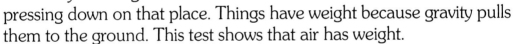

The air around presses against us equally in all directions. The pressure of the air in any place is caused by the weight of all the air pressing down on that place. Things have weight because gravity pulls them to the ground. This test shows that air has weight.

Tie a piece of string to the middle of a thin stick and hang the string from a hook. Blow up two identical balloons, making one bigger than the other. Tie one balloon on to each end of the stick. The end with the bigger balloon will dip down. It is heavier than the smaller balloon because it contains more air.

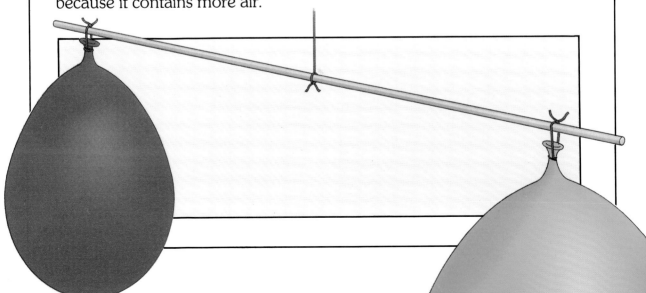

Upside-down Water

Hold a glass over a sink or a bowl and fill it right to the top with water. Carefully slide a smooth piece of card, such as a postcard, over the top. Hold your hand on the card and slowly turn the glass upside down. When you take away your hand, what happens?

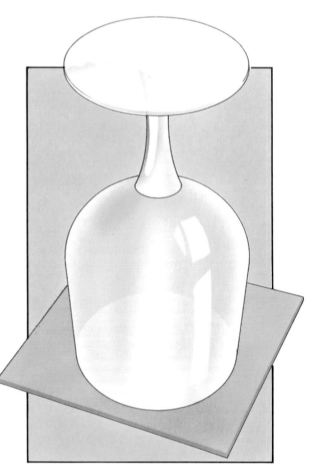

What happens
The air pushes against the card and should keep the water in the glass. The pressure of the air upwards is greater than the pressure of the water downwards.

 ## Make a Siphon

1. Fill two large jars with water. Hold some plastic tubing under water in a bowl until the air has escaped.
2. Pinch both tube ends and put one end under water in each jar. Lift one jar up and down.

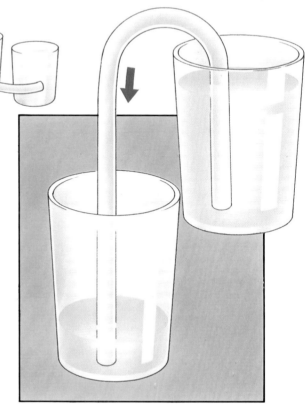

What happens
When one jar is lower than the other, the air pressing down on the water in the top jar will force the water up the tube, and down into the other jar.

Make a Balloon Rocket

You will need:
a balloon, a straw, strong sticky tape, scissors, strong thread.

1. Cut a straw in half and push one end of a long piece of thread through the straw.
2. Tie the thread tightly across a room.
3. Cut two pieces of sticky tape.
4. Blow a little air into the balloon.
5. Hold the end of the balloon tightly so the air cannot escape and ask a friend to help you tape the balloon firmly to the straw.
6. Blow some more air into the balloon.

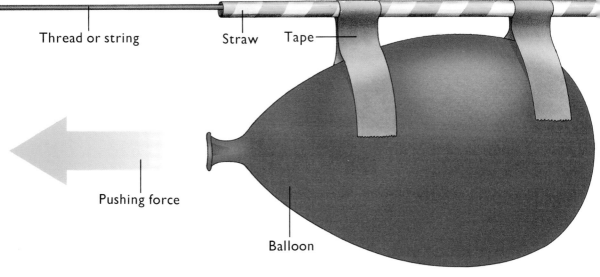

Thread or string   Straw   Tape

Pushing force

Balloon

7. When you let the balloon go, how fast does it travel? Can you think of a way of slowing down the rocket?
8. If you set up two balloon rockets side by side, you could have a race!

What happens
The air inside the balloon is squashed into a small space so it is at a high pressure. As it rushes out of the neck of the balloon, it pushes the balloon in the opposite direction. The hot gases rushing out of the back of a jet aeroplane push it forwards.

▲ Powerful fans on a hovercraft blow air under the craft, which increases the air pressure there. This higher pressure pushes the craft off the ground or water, so it floats on a cushion of compressed air. Propellers on the top of the hovercraft spin round to push the air aside and drive the hovercraft backwards or forwards.

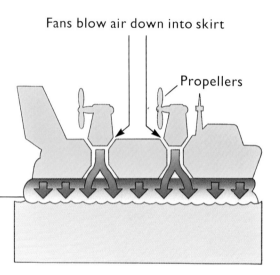

Fans blow air down into skirt

Propellers

Cushion of compressed air

WIND AND WEATHER

Weather is produced by air moving from place to place – which we call winds. Winds are caused by warm air rising and cooler air moving in to take its place. Warm air is lighter or less dense than cool air, so it creates low air pressure. Cool air is heavier or more dense and creates high air pressure. Usually we have fine weather when the air pressure is high. Low air pressure brings clouds, rain or snow.

▼ Winds can sometimes blow at tremendous speeds and cause great damage. The winds produced by a hurricane can travel at 120–160 kilometres an hour. This picture shows the damage from a hurricane in Darwin, Australia.

Make a Barometer

A barometer measures air pressure. A change in the air pressure tells us when the weather is likely to change.

You will need:
a tall, clear bottle, a saucer or dish, two thin pieces of wood, sticky tape, a pen.

1. Fill the bottle with water. Hold the saucer or dish over the top of the bottle and carefully turn the bottle upside down. Some of the water will spill out, so do this over a sink or a bowl.
2. Stand the saucer or dish with the bottle inside it in a cool place.
3. Tilt the bottle to let some air in. It needs to be about one-third full of air.
4. Slip the pieces of wood under the bottle to lift it clear of the saucer or dish. This lets water move in and out of the bottle.
5. Stick a long piece of tape on the side of the bottle and mark the level of the water.
6. Watch your barometer carefully and mark the level of the water at regular intervals. Can you predict the weather with your barometer?

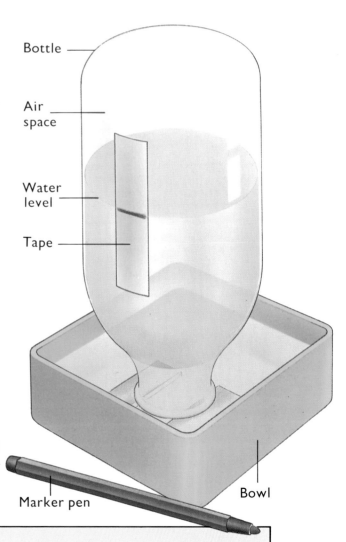

Bottle

Air space

Water level

Tape

Marker pen

Bowl

What happens
When the air pressure increases, it pushes down on the water in the dish, forcing the water up the bottle. When the air pressure falls, the level of water in the bottle falls too. Better weather will usually follow when the barometer rises and worse weather when it falls.

Make a Wind Sock

A wind sock at an airport shows the strength and direction of the wind and helps pilots to take off and land safely. Make a wind sock yourself.

1. Cut the shirt sleeve in half.
2. Ask an adult to help you bend the wire into a circle. Sew one end of the sleeve to the wire.
3. Tie a piece of string to one side of the circle.
4. Tie the string to a long pole, such as an old broom handle.
5. Put your wind sock outside.

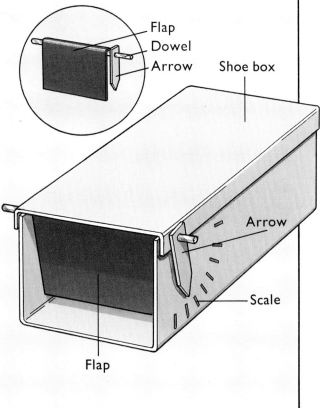

Wire loop
String
Nail
Broom handle

Flap
Dowel
Arrow
Shoe box
Arrow
Scale
Flap

Measuring Wind Speed

You will need:
a cardboard box, dowel, a pen, cardboard, tape.

1. Cut off both ends of the box.
2. Draw a scale at one end.
3. Make a cardboard flap which will fit inside one end of the box.
4. Stick the flap to the dowel and push the dowel through the sides of the box. Make sure the flap of card can swing freely.
5. Stick an arrow on to the dowel and put the wind speed measurer outside facing into the wind. How much does the flap move?

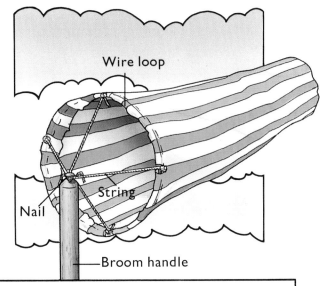

Make a Windmill

You will need:
a long strip of 1 cm square wood, card, empty box, glue, sticky tape, 2 cotton reels, corrugated card, thin dowel, card or cloth, scissors, hacksaw.

1. Cut two short lengths of the one centimetre square wood and ask an adult to help you drill a hole through the centre point of each piece of wood.

2. Cut two small circles of card and make a hole in the middle of each circle.

3. Push a thin piece of dowel through the hole in one piece of card, through the hole in the one centimetre square wood and out through the other card circle. Glue the dowel to fix the wood in a cross shape.

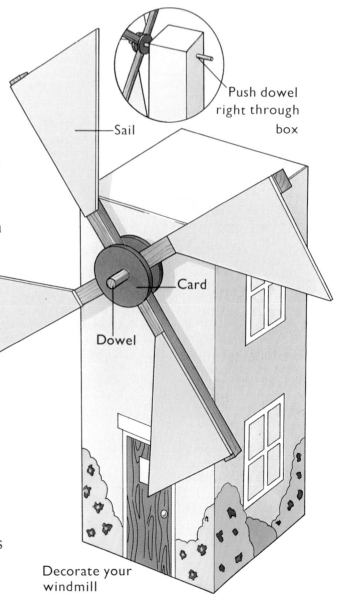

Card

Sail

Wood

Sail

Card

Push dowel through all holes and glue

Push dowel right through box

Sail

Card

Dowel

Decorate your windmill

4. Cut sails out of card or cloth and fix them to the wooden cross with glue or sticky tape.

5. Push the dowel through the top of the box.

6. Put your windmill in a breeze outside or on a windowsill.

7. Can you use your windmill to lift something? Hint: fix a cotton reel to the dowel at the back of the box.

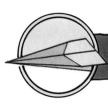

FLYING THINGS

How many flying things can you think of? Some flying things are alive. They are animals or parts of plants. Others are machines made by people.

You could make a scrapbook of flying things. Fill your scrapbook with drawings, postcards and pictures cut out of newspapers or magazines.

Can you make a piece of paper fly through the air? First, drop the paper from a height. As the sheet of paper falls, air is trapped underneath. As the air escapes, it makes the paper sway.

Fold the paper in half and open it out. Fold one of the long edges back. Drop the paper from a height again.

The centre fold makes the air pressure the same on both sides of the paper and this stops it rolling from side to side. Folding a long edge makes one side of the paper heavier, so the paper pushes through air more easily.

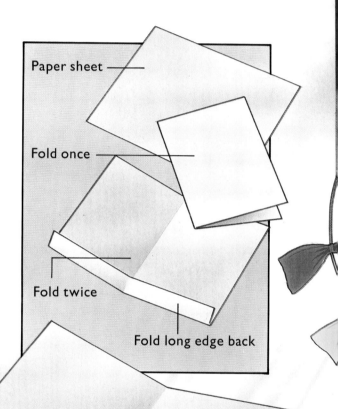

Paper sheet

Fold once

Fold twice

Fold long edge back

▲ Have you ever seen people hang gliding? As the wings of the glider move through the air, they help to lift the glider upwards. Warm air currents rising up from the ground also help to push the glider up into the sky.

Make a Frisbee

To find out more about how things move through the air, make a frisbee.

You will need:
thin balsa wood from a model shop (2–3 millimetres thick), elastic band, scissors, sandpaper, paints.

1. Use the scissors to cut two pieces of balsa wood about 2–3 centimetres wide by 12–20 centimetres long. The size of the pieces is not all that important so long as they are both the same size.
2. Rub the sandpaper over the wood to make it smooth on both sides.
3. Hold the two pieces of wood in a cross shape and wrap the elastic band round them to fix them in this position.
4. Paint your frisbee any colours you like.
5. Take your frisbee outside. Hold the tip of one piece of wood, lift the frisbee above your head and throw it into a breeze. Try to spin it as you

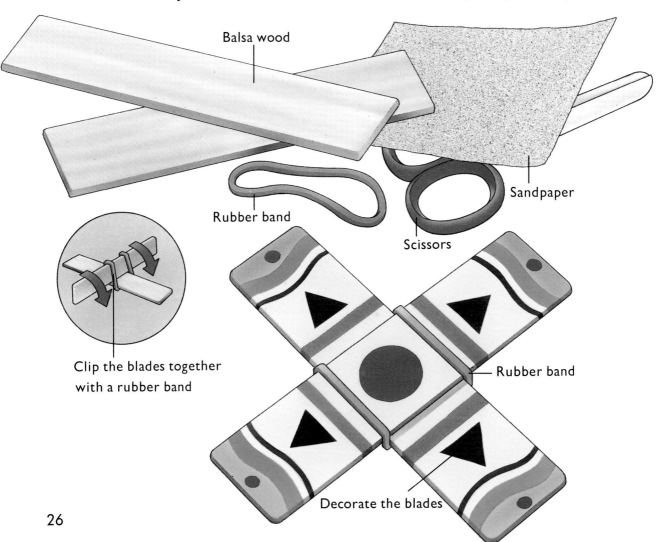

Balsa wood

Rubber band

Sandpaper

Scissors

Clip the blades together with a rubber band

Rubber band

Decorate the blades

throw. How far does it fly? If you round off the corners of the wood, does it fly further?
6. What happens if you fix the two pieces of wood so that one is standing up and the other lies flat?

▲ A gannet has a smooth, streamlined body shape, which helps it to fly fast through the air. You can find out more about birds and flight on pages 38–39.

What happens

As objects fly through the air, the air pulls against them and holds them back. This resistance to movement is called drag. Flying objects need enough energy to overcome drag and move through the air. By smoothing the wood with the sandpaper, you cut down the amount of drag. The frisbee with one piece of wood standing up creates a lot of air resistance and hardly flies at all. The flat frisbee creates less air resistance and flies much better.

Wings

Cut out a strip of paper about 20 centimetres long and 5 centimetres or more wide. Fold the paper into a bridge shape and put the bridge on a flat surface. Blow steadily under the bridge. What happens to the bridge?

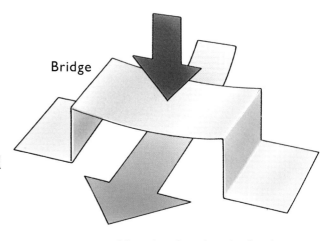

Bridge

Blow hard under the bridge

What happens

The top of the bridge moves down and the paper moves up. When air moves fast, it is at a low pressure. Because the air pressure under the bridge is low, the higher air pressure on top pushes the bridge down. This link between air speed and air pressure is very important. It helps all sorts of flying things, from swallows to aeroplanes, to fly.

Making Round Wings

1. Make a loop out of each strip of paper. Overlap the ends and tape them inside and outside the loop to match the picture.
2. Push the straw through the pockets in the loops.
3. How well does your straw plane fly? Put the loops on the top or the bottom of the straw and in different positions along the straw. How does this affect the way the plane flies? Does the plane fly better with the small or the large loop in front?

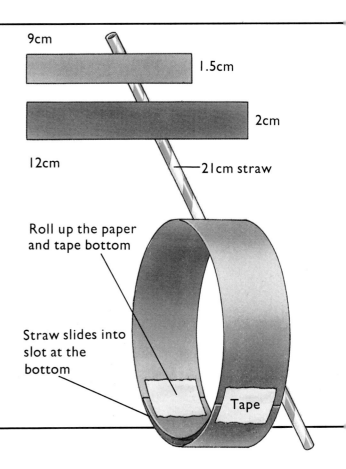

9cm

1.5cm

2cm

12cm

21cm straw

Roll up the paper and tape bottom

Straw slides into slot at the bottom

Tape

Make a Wing

A wing is a special shape called an aerofoil.

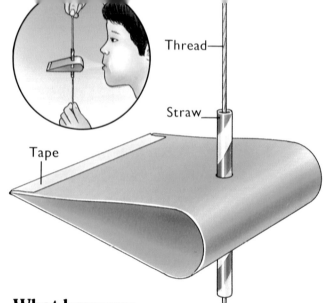

Thread

Straw

Tape

1. Cut a thin strip of paper about 4 cm wide and 26 cm long.
2. Cut a short length of straw.
3. Bend and fold the paper into a wing shape.
4. Use sticky tape to join the ends of the paper on top of the wing.
5. Push the straw through holes in the middle of the wing and fix it in place with tape.
6. Push a long piece of thread down through the straw.
7. Hold the thread and blow.

What happens

The air going over the top of the wing moves faster, and faster air means lower pressure. The slower air under the wing is at a higher pressure and pushes the wing up the thread. This upward pushing force is called lift.

What happens

The round wings on this plane work in the same way as flatter wings. The air moves more slowly under the wing and the higher air pressure lifts the plane up into the air.

Make Paper Gliders

Use A4-sized paper, about 30 centimetres by 20 centimetres. You can make paper gliders from different kinds of paper, such as newspaper, glossy magazine paper, crepe paper or tissue paper. What is the best kind of material for making paper gliders?

1. Fold the paper in half down the middle of the long side and open it out again.
2. Fold the top corners over so they meet in the middle.
3. Fold the same corners to the middle once more.
4. Turn the paper over.
5. Fold the sides to the middle and then fold the glider in half.
6. Grip the glider firmly by the centre fold and pull the wings flat.
7. Use sticky tape to hold the wings together in the middle.
8. Add one or more paper clips or a small piece of modelling clay to the nose of the glider. Does the glider fly better?
9. Cut some small flaps in the end of the wings. Bend the flaps up and down and see how this changes the direction the glider flies in. See pages 32–33.

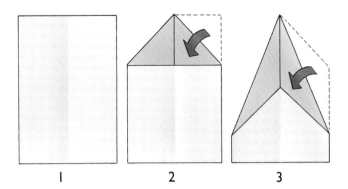

1 2 3

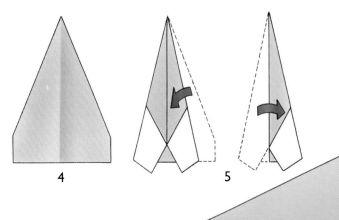

4 5

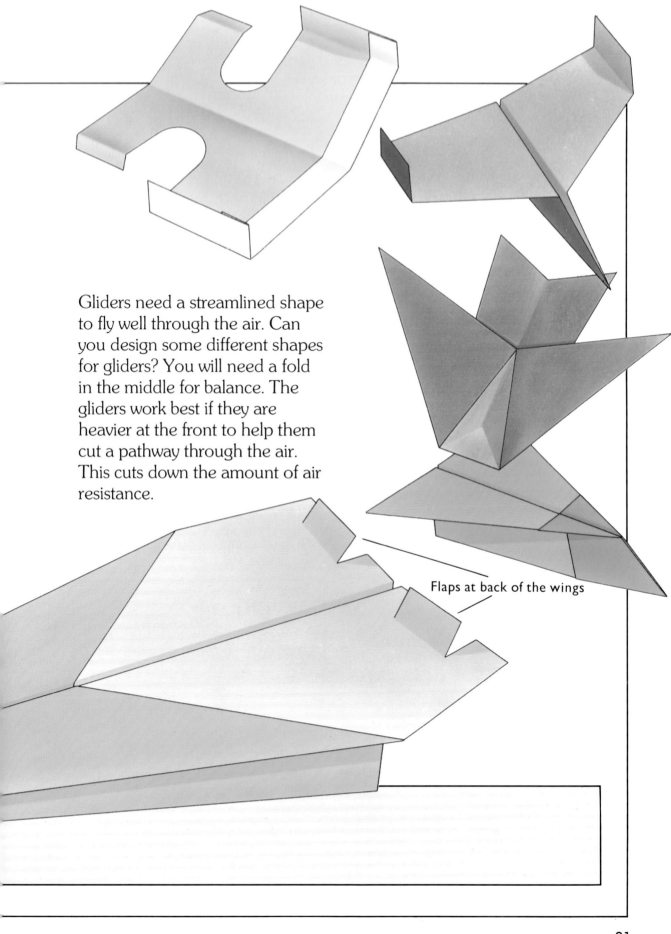

Gliders need a streamlined shape to fly well through the air. Can you design some different shapes for gliders? You will need a fold in the middle for balance. The gliders work best if they are heavier at the front to help them cut a pathway through the air. This cuts down the amount of air resistance.

Flaps at back of the wings

▲ To take off, a plane uses its engines to move fast along the runway. As it moves, air flows above and below the wings and produces lift. When there is enough lift to overcome the force of gravity, the plane takes off. In the air, the plane is slowed down by the resistance or drag of the air. The power of the engines has to overcome this dragging effect to keep the plane moving.

Making an Aeroplane

You will need:
a straw, paperclips, stiff paper, a pencil, sticky tape, scissors.

1. Make a wing shape, with the top edge curved, from a piece of stiff paper about 24 centimetres by 13 centimetres.
2. Tape the back edge of the wing and cut ailerons in this edge.
3. For the tail, cut a piece of stiff paper about 20 centimetres by 3.5 centimetres and fold the middle so it sticks up. Cut away about 1 centimetre of the flat pieces either side of the tail.
4. Cut elevators in the flat edges of the tail piece.
5. Use sticky tape to fix the wings and tail piece to the straw.
6. Weight the nose of the plane with several paperclips.

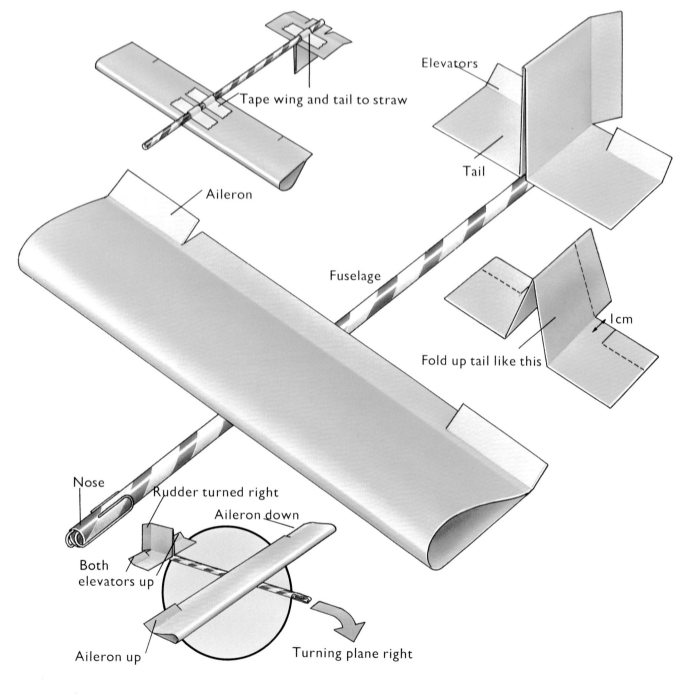

Tape wing and tail to straw

Elevators

Tail

Aileron

Fuselage

Fold up tail like this

1cm

Nose

Rudder turned right

Aileron down

Both elevators up

Aileron up

Turning plane right

7. Now bend the flaps up and down and the rudder from side to side to see how this affects the flight of the plane.

Have you ever noticed the flaps on the wings and tail piece of a passenger aeroplane? The flaps on the wings are called ailerons. The ones on the tail piece are called elevators. The pilot moves the ailerons and elevators, together with a tail flap called the rudder, to make the aeroplane turn, climb or dive through the air. Make your own aeroplane to see how this works.

Spinning Around

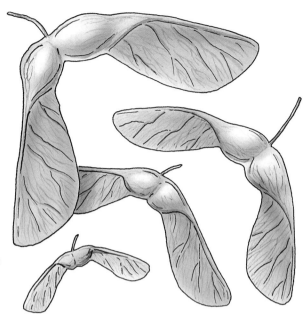

Have you ever watched a maple seed falling off a tree? As it spins round and round, the air rushing above and below the wing shape produces lift. This helps the seed to fly away from the parent tree. If it lands too near the parent, it is not likely to find enough space, light and water to grow into a new tree.

▼ Each one of the long, thin rotor blades on top of a helicopter is like the 'wing' of a maple seed. It is a long, narrow aerofoil. A helicopter stands still and turns its rotors to make air rush past its 'wings'. The faster the rotors spin, the faster the air moves and the more lift is produced.

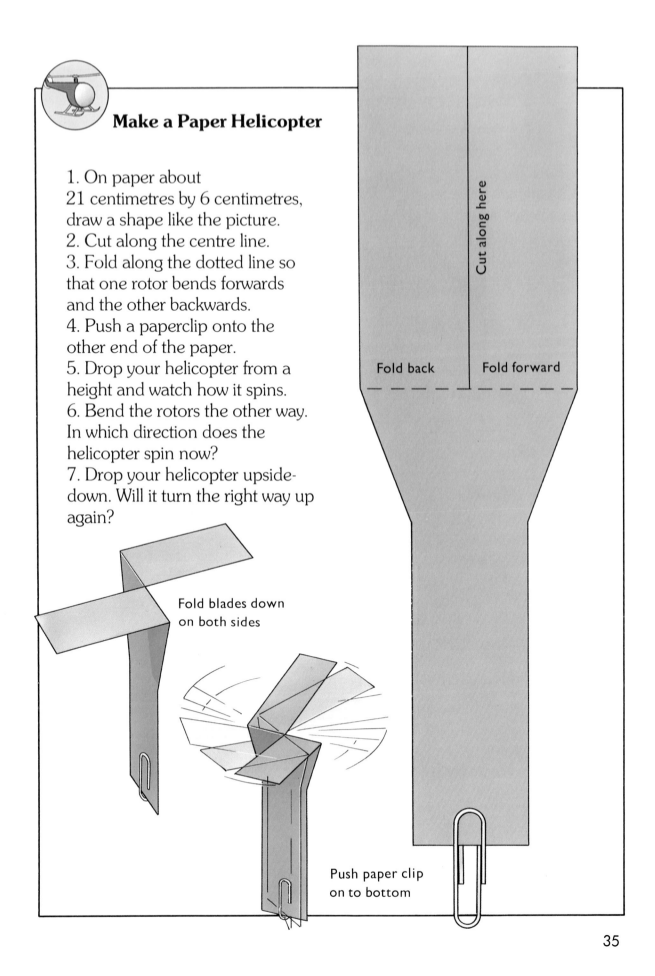

Make a Paper Helicopter

1. On paper about
21 centimetres by 6 centimetres,
draw a shape like the picture.
2. Cut along the centre line.
3. Fold along the dotted line so
that one rotor bends forwards
and the other backwards.
4. Push a paperclip onto the
other end of the paper.
5. Drop your helicopter from a
height and watch how it spins.
6. Bend the rotors the other way.
In which direction does the
helicopter spin now?
7. Drop your helicopter upside-
down. Will it turn the right way up
again?

Cut along here

Fold back

Fold forward

Fold blades down
on both sides

Push paper clip
on to bottom

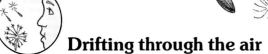

 Drifting through the air

Air resistance can sometimes be useful if we want to slow flying things down. For instance, parachutes slow down things falling down to the ground. A dandelion seed has a little parachute to help it drift slowly on the wind. This helps it to cover long distances and to move away from its parent plant.

Make Parachutes

> **You will need:**
> scissors, thread or string, different materials and loads.

1. Cut some squares out of different materials. Make the squares different sizes.
2. Use tape to fix thread or string to each corner of the squares.
3. Tie a load to the strings under each parachute, and launch it.
4. How long does each parachute take to fall down to the ground? Do larger parachutes fall more quickly or more slowly? If the parachute is carrying a heavy load, does this make a difference?
5. Make a small hole in the top of one of the parachutes. How does this affect the way it falls down?

What happens
The force of gravity pulls the parachute down to the ground. But some air is trapped under the parachute. This air gets squashed, pushes up against the parachute and makes it fall more slowly.

▲ Modern parachutes have a hole in the top. This helps the air trapped inside the parachute to escape more smoothly and stops the parachute from wobbling and swaying as it falls through the air.

▶ Some animals, such as this colugo, have flaps of skin along the sides of the body. When they spread out this skin, they can glide through the air like living parachutes. The colugo can glide as far as 135 metres between trees.

The first flying animals on Earth were probably insects. About 200 million years ago, winged reptiles called pterosaurs flew in the skies above the dinosaurs. The wings of pterosaurs were made of skin stretched between their arms and legs, rather like the wings of the bats alive today. The largest pterosaurs had wings that were as big as a small aeroplane.

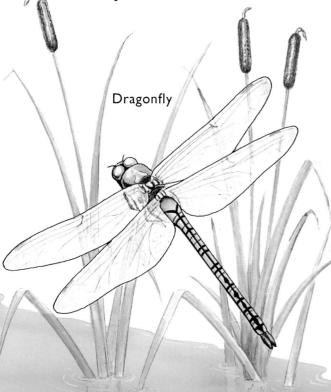

Dragonfly

Nowadays, only birds, bats and insects have wings to power flight upwards instead of just gliding along. Being able to fly is very useful. It helps animals to escape from danger as well as find food and places to nest.

Insects have very thin, flat wings with powerful muscles. As they flap their wings, they push against the air and this makes them move upwards and forwards. Flies can beat their wings as fast as 1000 times a second.

▲ As a bird's wings beat downwards, they create more air pressure under the wings. This extra pressure pushes the bird upwards. When the wings are pulled up again, the tips of the feathers move apart to let air flow through.

▼ Hummingbirds are like tiny helicopters. They can fly sideways, backwards and even upside-down. Hummingbirds beat their wings between 22 and 78 times a second and can fly up to 65 kilometres per hour.

Birds are well designed living flying machines. Their body is light in weight and some of their bones are hollow to reduce weight. Their feathers fit closely together to give them a smooth, streamlined shape. And their front arms have become wings. A bird's wing is shaped like an aerofoil to give it lift. Birds have very powerful chest muscles to beat their wings up and down.